IN THE

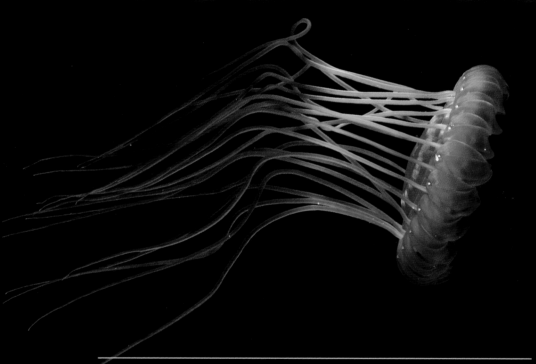

BY SNEED B. COLLARD III

 **Marshall Cavendish**
Benchmark
New York

To Edie, Tammy, and Dave,
For unlocking the magic of our planet
and taking me on the adventure of a lifetime.
—Sneed

ACKNOWLEDGMENTS

With special thanks to Dr. Edith Widder, director of the Bioluminescence Department of the Harbor Branch Oceanographic Institution, Fort Pierce, Florida, for giving me the opportunity to share the world of bioluminescence firsthand; also for her helpful reading of the manuscript and for providing many of the images of those splendid luminescent critters. Thanks, too, to Professor James Case for his comments and suggestions on the manuscript.

Marshall Cavendish Benchmark
99 White Plains Road
Tarrytown, New York 10591-9001
www.marshallcavendish.us

Copyright © 2006 by Sneed B. Collard III

All Internet sites were available and accurate when this book was sent to press.

Library of Congress Cataloging-in-Publication Data
Collard, Sneed B.
In the deep sea / by Sneed B. Collard III.
p. cm. — (Science adventures)
Summary: "Describes the work of Dr. Edith Widder and other biologists in
the field of bioluminescence research"—Provided by publisher.
Includes bibliographical references and index.
ISBN 0-7614-1952-7
Bioluminescence—Juvenile literature. I. Title. II. Series.
QH641.C65 2005
572'.4358—dc22   2004026489

Series design by Anne Scatto / PIXEL PRESS

Art Research by Rose Corbett Gordon, Mystic CT

Front and back cover images: Edith Widder/HBOI

Illustration page 30 by Christopher Santoro

Page i, 2, 4, 5, 6, 9 bottom, 13, 14, 15, 20, 21, 22, 25, 27, 28, 32: Edith Widder/HBOI; pages iv, 8: Tom Smoyer/HBOI; pages 9 top, 34: Norbert Wu/Peter Arnold, Inc.; page 16: Foto-Unep/Peter Arnold, Inc.; page 18: Steve Haddock/MBARI; page 36: Qinetiq/Peter Arnold, Inc.

Printed in Malaysia
135642

FRONT COVER: A viperfish, *Chauliodus sloani*, one of hundreds of ocean animals that can make its own light.
BACK COVER: The bioluminescent suckers of the octopus *Stauroteuthis syrtensis*.
TITLE PAGE: *Atolla wyvillei*, one of many jelly animals that makes its own light.

Contents

Introduction

Humans are only beginning to understand the richness and complexity of life on Earth. Every day, scientists are making new, startling discoveries about the wonderful planet we call home. This series seeks to share the lives and adventures of a few of these scientists as they probe the mysteries of places as diverse as coral reefs, rain forests, and the deep sea.

In the Deep Sea follows Dr. Edith Widder as she dives into the ocean depths to learn about bioluminescence—light made by living species. I first met Dr. Widder more than twenty years ago. Since that time, she has become one of the world's experts on bioluminescence. Recently, I experienced the thrill of a lifetime when Dr. Widder invited me on two deep-sea dives off the coast of the Bahama Islands. As our submersible descended 3,000 feet to the ocean floor, I understood why Dr. Widder is so passionate about science and why she is so enchanted with bioluminescence. I hope that, after reading this book, you will too.

OPPOSITE: Dr. Edith Widder, one of the world's experts on bioluminescence, gets ready to explore the ocean depths.

1

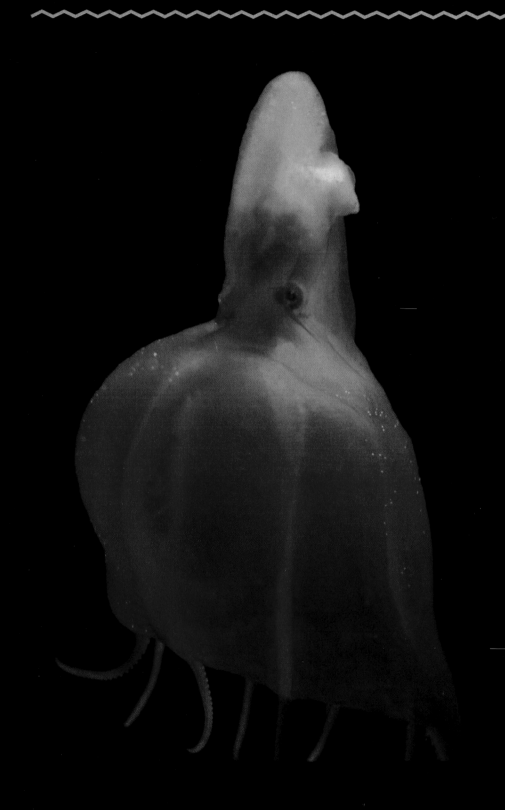

Suckers and Submarines

N 1997, DR. EDITH WIDDER was diving off the Gulf of Maine in a deep-sea submersible called the Johnson-Sea-Link. Dr. Widder was using the four-person submersible to study *bioluminescent* animals—those that can make their own light. In the submersible, she and the pilot searched for bioluminescent shrimp and jellylike animals that lived more than 2,000 feet below the ocean surface. As the pilot guided the Johnson-Sea-Link through the deep, dark waters, however, Dr. Widder suddenly spotted a beautiful football-sized red octopus called *Stauroteuthis syrtensis.*

Dr. Widder asked the pilot to try to capture the octopus using one of the Plexiglas "buckets" mounted on the front of the submersible—not an easy task! Catching animals with the sub, in fact, was a lot like trying to catch a butterfly using a net taped to the front of a pickup truck. The submersible's pilot, though, expertly maneuvered the Sea-Link into the

OPPOSITE: The ghostlike *Stauroteuthis syrtensis* is one of several species of octopuses adapted for deep ocean life.

3

right position. With a last upward thrust of the sub, the octopus slid into one of the buckets, and with a flick of a switch, the pilot closed the lids.

When they returned to the surface, a huge crane lifted the Johnson-Sea-Link out of the water and onto the deck of its 200-foot support ship. Once the deck crew bolted the submersible securely in place, Dr. Widder climbed out and carried the bucket containing the living octopus into the ship's lab. With one of her colleagues, Sönke Johnsen, looking over her shoulder, Dr. Widder began taking pictures of the remarkable animal. As Dr. Widder fired off one picture after

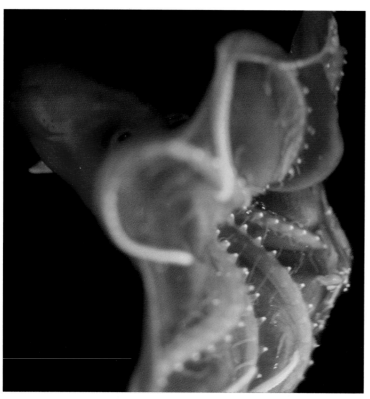

The suckers of *Stauroteuthis* do not function like the suckers of most other octopuses. Amazingly, they have evolved into light organs. This is how *Stauroteuthis* appears with the lights on.

another, Sönke Johnsen said, "You know, those don't look like suckers on the octopus's arms."

Dr. Widder took a closer look at the animal's suckers and said, "You know, you're right."

Then, together, the two scientists exclaimed, "They look like light organs!"

The two whisked the octopus into another room, and turned off the lights. As their eyes adjusted to the darkness, they looked at the octopus. To their amazement, the scientists saw that the animal's suckers glowed with a beautiful blue light.

When Dr. Widder and Sönke Johnsen reported their discovery in the scientific journal *Nature,* biologists all over the world got excited. Not only was *Stauroteuthis syrtensis* the first octopus ever discovered to have bioluminescent suckers, but those suckers provided important clues for how—and why—bioluminescence has evolved in ocean animals.

This is how *Stauroteuthis* appears with the lights off.

Got Light?

Dr. Widder is not the first person to be enthralled by bioluminescence. Few people who've watched a firefly flash on a summer's evening ever forget the enchantment of the insect's magical light. However, only a handful of people—including scientists—realize the extent to which bioluminescence influences life on our planet, especially in the ocean. On land, bioluminescence has evolved in several hundred species of fireflies and a few other animals, bacteria, and fungi. In the ocean, the number of bioluminescent species soars into the *thousands*. These species belong to almost every group of ocean creatures, from the

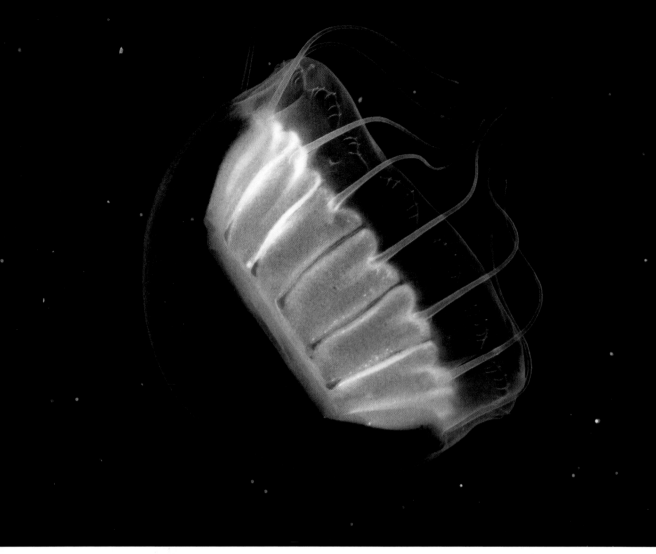

smallest worms and single-celled organisms to larger octopuses, fishes, and shrimps.

Why have so few people noticed? One problem is the way scientists have studied the ocean. For hundreds of years, the main way people have investigated the deep sea is by lowering nets down into it. The problem with nets is that they rip apart many fragile ocean animals and are too slow to catch many others. As a result, scientists have been able to catch and examine only a fraction of deep-sea animals.

An even bigger problem is that for humans, the deep sea is a very hostile place. It's dark, cold, and under intense pressure that would crush most human beings. The deep sea also has no air to breathe. Even with scuba gear, humans can only dive a couple hundred feet at most. To go deeper just hasn't been possible.

Until recently.

Enter the Deep

People began experimenting with submarines for military use in the mid-nineteenth century and steadily perfected these machines after World War I. Most military submarines are large and bulky, however, and don't easily lend themselves to scientific research. Also, most military subs do not dive deeper than a couple thousand feet.

Starting in the 1960s, though, scientists began building smaller devices known as submersibles. These watercraft can go to great depths. They are powered by batteries, however, and so must rely on a "mother ship," from which they are launched and to which they return to have their batteries recharged. One of the first submersibles was *Alvin,* a three-person craft that could carry scientists down 6,000 feet. Since then, researchers from different countries have built a number of other submersibles— some capable of traveling several miles beneath the ocean surface. By visiting the deep sea directly in these craft, scientists have made remarkable discoveries about the ocean and marine life. Many also have witnessed the incredible variety of bioluminescent animals that inhabit the deep.

The Johnson-Sea-Link is one of several submersibles that Dr. Widder has used to study deep-sea bioluminescence.

Dr. Widder, however, has been one of the few scientists to recognize the importance of bioluminescence to deep-sea life. She's also been one of the only biologists to use deep-sea submersibles to study bioluminescent animals in their own environment. The discoveries that she and a few other scientists have made have truly "shed light" on bioluminescence and its role in the deep sea.

Where Does the Light Come From?

Bioluminescence is created when a chemical called a luciferin reacts with oxygen and an enzyme called a luciferase. The molecular structures of luciferins and luciferases differ in different organisms. Most bioluminescent animals make the luciferins and luciferases themselves, and the light is produced in their skin or in special light organs called photophores. Other animals steal and use light-producing chemicals from bioluminescent animals that they eat. Quite a few animals harbor bioluminescent bacteria in their bodies and use the light made by these bacteria for their own purposes.

For example, the "flashlight fish" (Photoblepharon palpebratus) keeps glowing bacteria in a sac beneath its eyes. To turn the light on and off, the fish opens and closes a shutter—like an eyelid—that covers up this sac.

The flashlight fish has a light organ beneath its eye. It doesn't make light-producing chemicals itself, however. Instead, this organ is filled with tiny bioluminescent bacteria.

Many animals manufacture their own light-producing chemicals that are stored in light organs called photophores.

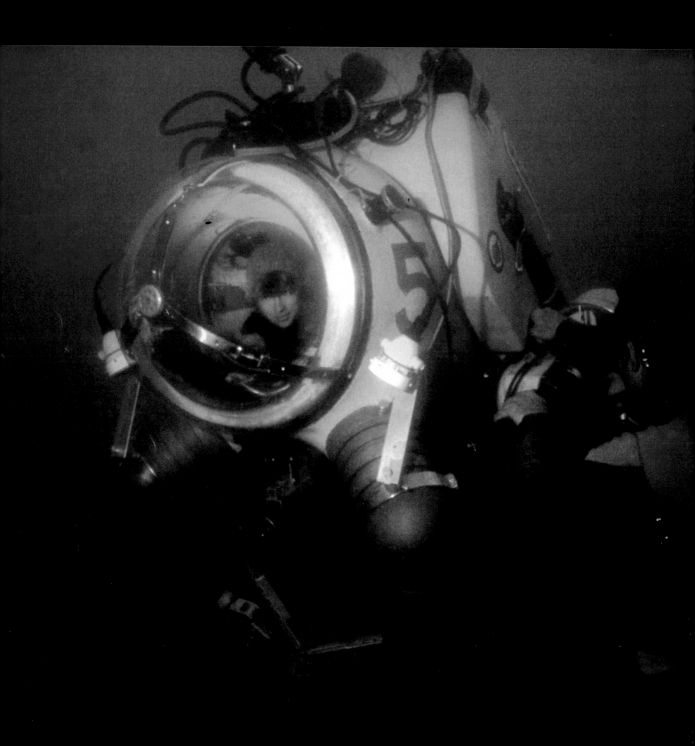

Diving into Science

DR. WIDDER, OR "EDIE," didn't begin her career studying bio-luminescence. If things had been a little different, she might not have become a biologist at all.

Edie grew up as the daughter of two mathematics professors in Boston. When she was eleven years old, her parents spent a year traveling around the world and took Edie with them. They started their trip in England and then traveled on to Sweden, Italy, and Egypt. After Egypt they spent six months in Australia and, on their way home, stopped in Fiji, a group of islands in the Pacific Ocean.

"It was quite a formative year for me," Edie explains. "When we saw the paintings and sculptures in England and Rome, I thought I wanted to be an artist. When we saw the pyramids of Egypt, I thought

OPPOSITE: Edie first entered the world of the deep in the diving submersible WASP.

I wanted to be an archaeologist. And it just sort of progressed that way. Then, when I got to Australia, I began climbing trees after koalas and in Fiji, I got to explore a coral reef for the first time."

After visiting Australia and Fiji, Edie decided that art and archaeology were out. She wanted to study living things.

Professional Twists and Turns

All through high school, Edie pursued an interest in marine biology. She realized, though, that jobs in marine biology were few and far between. Instead, while studying at Tufts University in Boston, she decided to major in physiology—the study of respiration, reproduction, and other essential body functions. Afterwards, she earned a master's degree in biochemistry at the University of California at Santa Barbara, and then found herself working on her PhD, or doctorate degree, in the laboratory of Professor James F. Case.

It was in Case's lab that Edie first became acquainted with bioluminescence. For her PhD research project, Edie studied a tiny single-celled organism called a *dinoflagellate*. As she worked, Edie was amazed at how complex the dinoflagellate's behavior seemed to be—especially how it could make and use light. Still, Edie's interests centered more on biochemistry and physiology than on light.

After finishing her PhD, Edie continued working in Case's lab. One day, the lab received an instrument called an optical multi-channel analyzer. The multi-channel analyzer could instantaneously measure the wavelengths of light coming from any kind of light source, even a very dim one. "I've always been a gadget freak," Edie says. "And so I just started playing around with this multi-channel analyzer. Dr. Case saw me using it and said, 'Maybe you should take this thing to sea and we should start measuring bioluminescence from animals.'"

Soon, Edie found herself on ships, measuring the light made by deep-sea animals that were brought up in nets. It wasn't long before she would be descending into the ocean's depths herself. On her second

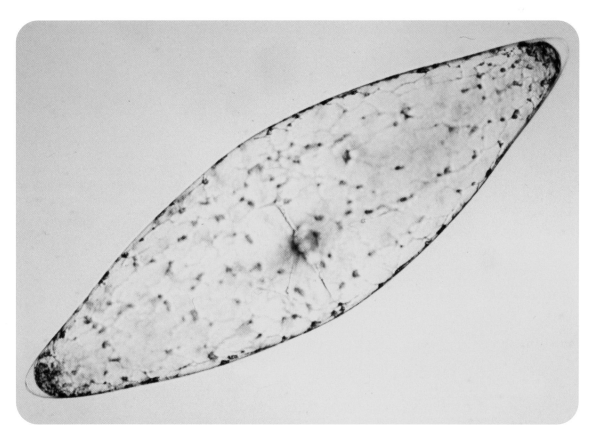

The first bioluminescent organism Edie studied was the single-celled dinoflagellate.

cruise, Edie met scientists who were using a deep-sea diving device called WASP. WASP could take a person down to 2,000 feet, and Edie eagerly wondered what the WASP pilots were getting to see. Recognizing Edie's enthusiasm, the chief scientist said, "Well, if you stay around for a year, I can probably get you trained as a WASP pilot and you can go down for yourself."

Edie dove at the chance.

Deep Pilot

Over the next few years, Edie trained as a pilot for WASP and a deep-sea submersible called *Deep Rover*. Diving in these submersibles turned her scientific interests upside down. Instead of studying the ocean only from animals brought up in nets, Edie now observed the deep sea in person. As she bobbed and floated through the depths, she saw strange fish with big eyes and large teeth. She saw fantastic, beautiful jellies hanging and swimming through the dark waters. And she saw

This black devil anglerfish is one of many bizarre deep-sea fish Edie met on her early dives.

14

one thing that impressed her more than anything else: light.

"It was like being in the middle of a fireworks display that was just breathtaking," Edie recalls. "I'd see things that looked like little puffs of blue smoke. Blue sparkles—like fairy dust—would shoot up out of the submersible's thrusters like you'd thrown a log on a campfire. Pyrotechnics of sparks were flowing everywhere!"

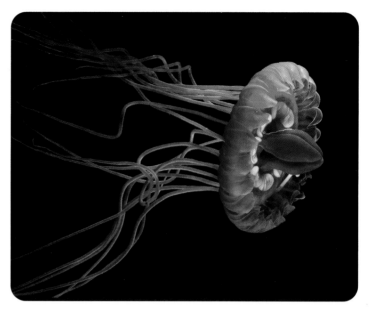

Beautiful jellies such as *Atolla wyvillei* abound in the dark waters of the deep sea.

As she marveled at the display, a question lit up her brain. "You know," Edie thought to herself, "this has got to be one of the most important things in the ocean. Why aren't more people studying this?" It was a question that would set the course of Dr. Widder's career.

When bumped, this bioluminescent comb jelly erupts into a spectacular "fireworks display."

The Deep
Where and Why

VER SINCE HER FIRST DIVES in WASP and *Deep Rover*, Edie has dedicated herself to answering two questions: *Where* do deep-sea animals live, and *why* do so many of them make light?

Edie determined that the only way she could ever answer these questions was to study marine animals in their natural habitats. Unfortunately, using submersibles was expensive. How could she ever afford to do it? Soon, Edie found a way.

In 1989, Edie landed a job as a biologist at the Harbor Branch Oceanographic Institution—an institution established by the Johnson family of the Johnson & Johnson pharmaceutical company. This private institute had excellent facilities for biological research. Even more important, it owned and operated the two deep-sea submersibles known as the Johnson-Sea-Links. Operating the submersibles and

OPPOSITE: The ocean's roar has always captured people's imaginations. Exploring the mysteries beneath the waves, however, is the special role of the scientist.

17

their mother ships cost thousands of dollars per day, but as a Harbor Branch biologist, Edie would receive a couple of weeks of free dive time each year. Edie was delighted. Her opportunity for deep-sea research had arrived.

Deep Basics

One of the remarkable things about the ocean is how little we know about it. The ocean covers 70 percent of the earth's surface. Because it is three-dimensional, it makes up an even higher percentage of the living space on this planet. Yet in many ways, we know less about the ocean than we do about the moon. On land, for instance, we have a pretty good idea where bears and birds and insects and other animals live. In the ocean, we often don't have a clue. That's because the nets that collect animals usually jumble species together from different depths and places.

One of Edie's research goals was to try to figure out more precisely where ocean animals live, especially between the depths of 600 and 3,000 feet. Because so many of the animals living in this zone are bioluminescent, Edie decided she would try to use bioluminescence to identify which animals live where.

In one of her first studies, Edie attached a three-foot-wide round screen with a wide mesh to the outside of a Johnson-Sea-Link submersible. She focused a video camera on the screen. Then, during a dive, Edie instructed the pilot to go forward in a straight line at a slow speed. As the submersible moved forward, animals hit the screen and lit up, and their light patterns were recorded by the video camera. Edie

repeated the process at different depths and places until she had a whole series of video-tapes.

Living Profiles

Back at Harbor Branch, Edie figured out how to identify each animal species by the pattern of light it made when it hit the screen. She fed this information into a computer and used the computer to analyze her videotapes. As each animal hit the screen, the computer identified it and recorded it. Soon, Edie got an entire profile of which animal species live at different depths. It was the first time anyone had ever performed such a detailed profile of bioluminescent—or any other—deep-sea animals.

What did she find?

In the Gulf of Maine, Edie found that bioluminescent animals were not distributed evenly from the surface down to the bottom. Instead, they gathered in layers. In the space between these layers, the numbers of animals were low. In the layers themselves, however, thousands of animals packed together. Two of the most abundant were a shrimplike creature called a *euphausiid* and a kind of jelly animal called a *ctenophore.*

Edie made another discovery as well: different animals could be found at different depths during the 24-hour day. During daylight

Shrimplike euphausiids offered Edie clues to solving the mystery of bioluminescence.

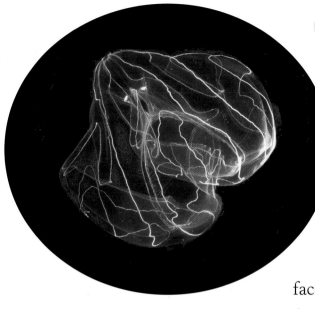

Like euphausiids, ctenophores turned out to have a migration pattern. Each night they move from deep to shallower waters.

hours, the euphausiids and ctenophores stayed at a depth of about 700 feet. But at night, the euphausiids migrated up to within 100 feet of the ocean surface—a migration pattern that turned out to be common to many bioluminescent animals. Edie and other biologists were intrigued by these patterns. Might they offer a clue to why bioluminescence evolved and how it helped inhabitants of the deep?

Why Light?

THE EVOLUTION OF BIOLUMINESCENCE is no accident. Scientists believe that the ability to make light has evolved *at least* thirty separate times in different animal groups over the past several hundred million years. That fact tells scientists that light is clearly important to how animals survive in the ocean. But how, and why, did the ability to make light come about?

Before answering these questions, it helps to understand how animals came to live in the darker waters of the deep sea in the first place. By piecing together clues from the bodies and behaviors of today's animals, Edie and other scientists believe that the ancestors of many of today's deep-sea animals evolved close to the ocean surface. Here, there was a lot of sunlight and a lot of food. Many animals evolved good eyes that helped them catch prey, identify predators, and observe mates and rivals.

As the shallow zones of the ocean became more and more crowded, however, danger from predators and competition for food increased. To

OPPOSITE: The light on the head stalk of a deep-sea anglerfish tricks prey into coming close enough to be captured.

23

avoid this danger and competition, many animals began moving ever deeper into the ocean. Some—like the euphausiids Edie studies—stayed deep only during the daylight hours and returned to the surface to hunt under the cover of darkness. Others took up permanent residence in the deep. Either way, life was harder for these animals because there wasn't as much light or food. Over time, though, some species developed new features, or *adaptations*, that helped them survive. Perhaps the greatest adaptation was the ability to make light.

A New Kind of Sucker

If you are an animal living in a dark world, being able to make your own light can help you in many ways. Edie's octopus, *Stauroteuthis syrtensis*, with its glowing suckers, is a wonderful example of the benefits of bio-luminescence. By studying its suckers, scientists think they understand how and why the ability to make light may have evolved in this animal.

Edie believes that *Stauroteuthis syrtensis*, like most octopuses, used to live on shallow ocean bottoms, where it used its suckers to cling to rocks and capture prey. During mating, males held their suckers over their heads to advertise to females, as many bottom-dwelling octopuses still do today. Over thousands—perhaps millions—of years, however, *Stauroteuthis* left the shallow sea bottom and moved into the open waters of the darker deep sea. Here, it may have found less competition for food or fewer predators, and it no longer needed its suckers for grabbing on to things.

It did still need its suckers for signaling to and attracting mates, however. The problem was that in dark water, it would be almost impossible for another octopus to see its suckers. Evolution, though, solved this problem. At some point a mutation, or change, occurred in the octopus's DNA. Mutations happen all the time in living organisms. Most are not helpful, and many actually hurt the animals they occur in. This mutation, though, was a helpful mutation because it caused the octopus's suckers to glow. Now, even in the dark depths, the octopus could hold its glowing suckers over its head and attract other octopuses to mate with.

Edie believes that the glowing suckers of *Stauroteuthis* serve to signal potential mates and attract prey.

But that wasn't the end of the story. As often happens, one adaptation led to another. The lights from the octopus's suckers happened to attract thousands of little animals called *copepods*. Edie believes that instead of chasing down its prey, as other octopuses do, *Stauroteuthis* began spreading out its glowing, webbed arms and attracting copepods close to its mouth. As the animals came in, the octopus trapped them in the "balloon" of its arms and devoured them. Over time, the glowing suckers probably evolved to a size and shape that would best attract the copepods. Eventually, what started out as a chance mutation—the ability to produce light—led to a whole new way of life for *Stauroteuthis.*

Burglar Alarms

Stauroteuthis syrtensis is only one amazing example of how marine animals use their bioluminescence. Another is to dial 9-1-1.

When Edie began diving in submersibles, one thing she noticed right away was that most deep-sea bioluminescent animals only rarely turned on their lights. While her sub was moving—and animals were bumping into it—lights were flashing on all around her. As soon as her craft stopped moving, though, the world went black. Why, she wondered, would this be? Why would millions of animals be sitting down there in complete darkness when they could be making their own light?

Edie and other scientists think that the answer is simple: if you light up, you call attention to yourself—attention you may not want. In a dark world full of predators, any bright light may attract a number of hungry mouths. That's why bioluminescent animals use their lights sparingly. Some use them only when hunting prey or attracting mates. Many only light up when it's a matter of life or death.

"The last resort for a lot of animals is something called the Burglar Alarm," Edie explains. "When an animal gets caught in the clutches of a predator, its only hope for escape is to attract the attention of something bigger and nastier that will eat what's trying to eat the first animal. That's what fear screams are in monkeys and birds. It's the burglar alarm—and it's why you should scream if you're being mugged.

"When they're being attacked," Edie continues, "a lot of animals use

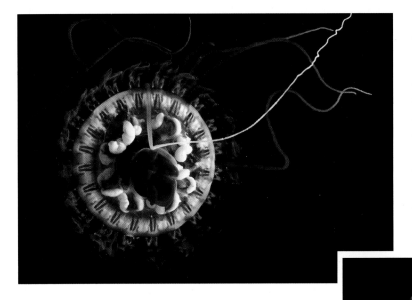

every light they've got and fire it off as brightly as possible to attract the attention of a predator."

Edie has discovered that the burglar alarms of some deep-sea jellies are particularly astonishing. She's found that when they are attacked, these animals light up in an astonishing display of "fireworks," with dazzling lights flashing on and off and back and forth in circular patterns. One of Edie's favorite animals, a deep-sea cucumber called *Enypniastes,* takes the burglar alarm a step further. When a predator comes into contact with *Enypniastes,* the sea cucumber's outer skin not only glows brightly, but sheds and sticks to the predator. This turns the would-be attacker into a brilliant target for every other hunter in the area. It's not surprising that few, if any, predators tangle with *Enypniastes.*

CHAPTER 5

Firefleas, Midshipmen, and Cookie Cutters

THOUGH EDIE IS ONE OF today's leading scientists studying bioluminescence, she is not the only one. Biologist James Morin, for example, has made fascinating discoveries about a group of tiny ocean animals called ostracods, or "firefleas."

On land, the largest group of bioluminescent animals—the fireflies—use their light primarily to identify and communicate with other fireflies. Male and female fireflies, scientists have learned, can distinguish members of their own species from other species by the number and length of their flashes.

OPPOSITE: A group of ostracods glows in the dark in the picture below. The photo above shows how these little "firefleas" appear with the lights on.

Evenly spaced horizontal signals

Vertical
signals
released
closer
and
closer
together

Rapid, flashing
displays by
groups of
ostracods

Studying communication in marine animals, however, has been much more difficult. Even using submersibles and scuba gear, it's almost impossible to spend enough time underwater to learn how bioluminescent animals communicate using their lights. In the 1980s, however, Jim Morin succeeded in conducting a long-term study of ostracods.

Ostracods are clam-shaped shrimplike animals with very good eyes. There are more than 7,500 species, and most live on the bottom of oceans or lakes. About 50 species are bioluminescent, and they seem to use their ability to make light in a remarkable way.

When it's time to mate, male ostracods rise up off the bottom and begin releasing little blobs of glowing substance in distinct patterns. Some ostracods release four to seven glowing spots in a vertical line, the first two lights far apart, and the last few closer together. Other ostracods release dozens of lights parallel to the bottom in something that looks like a jet's vapor trail. Some males "flash" together in a group.

Amazingly, Dr. Morin found, each species of ostracod has its own individual flash or "blob" pattern. What is the purpose of these different patterns? Dr. Morin concluded that, just like fireflies, female ostracods recognize males of their own species by the light patterns they see. In this way, many species of ostracods can live in the same area and mate only with their own kind.

OPPOSITE: About 50 species of ostracods are bioluminescent. Each species has its own individual flash pattern. Here are just three examples of how firefleas light up to attract their mates.

Now You See Me, Now You Don't

Much of our knowledge of bioluminescence has been pioneered in the laboratory of Professor James F. Case—Edie Widder's PhD professor. Professor Case has not only conducted hundreds of experiments himself on terrestrial and marine bioluminescence, but has trained many other leading research scientists.

One animal Professor Case has been studying is a fish called the plainfin midshipman, *Porichthys notatus.* During the day, this fish stays buried in sandy ocean bottoms. At dusk, it rises up into the water column to feed on plankton. One of the many interesting things about the midshipman is that its bottom, or ventral, side is covered with tiny light organs, or photophores. For many years, scientists have speculated on how the midshipman might be using these light organs. Are they

The midshipman's photophores allow it to "counterilluminate," or blend in with background light from the surface.

to attract mates? To attract prey? To warn predators of the midshipman's dangerous spines? The theory that seemed most likely to Professor Case is that the photophores provide a kind of camouflage called *counterillumination.*

To test this theory, Professor Case and a graduate student, R. D. Harper, placed a midshipman fish in an aquarium. They installed a camera beneath the aquarium and an adjustable light source above it. As they increased the light above the fish, the scientists watched what happened to the fish's photophores. It turned out that as the light above it increased, the fish increased the intensity of its own photophores to match! In other words, to a predator looking up, the midshipman camouflaged itself almost perfectly against the light coming down from the ocean surface.

Case and Harper's experiment provided a clear demonstration that many bioluminescent animals use their lights as camouflage. The midshipman is not the only animal that protects itself this way. Shrimps, squids, and many other marine animals use their photophores for counterillumination. In an open ocean where there's no place to hide, counterillumination helps level the playing field between predators and prey.

Cookie Cutters

Often it takes several scientists, working at different times and places, to understand bioluminescence and piece together how animals use it. The cookie cutter shark is a small shark about a foot and a half long that lives in the open ocean. It was first described in 1840 by a scientist named F. D. Bennett, who noted that the shark's ventral side glowed—a lot like the ventral side of the midshipman fish. Subsequently, other biologists figured out that the cookie cutter made its living by attack-

ing larger prey such as fast-moving tuna, dolphins, and walruses. Somehow, the cookie cutter glommed on to these animals and used its sawlike jaws to carve out round chunks of flesh. It also devoured large squids whole.

For scientists, the question was "How?" Cookie cutter sharks move very slowly through the water. How could they attack lightning-fast tuna and squid? Edie Widder stumbled onto the final piece of the puzzle when she took a closer look at the shark's bioluminescence.

Edie solved the puzzle of the cookie cutter shark by focusing on the fact that this predator has no photophores around its neck.

Like the midshipman fish, the cookie cutter counterilluminates. Thousands of photophores cover its ventral side, making it blend in with light coming down from the ocean surface. What puzzled Edie was that there were no photophores around the shark's neck. To a large predator looking up from below, the cookie cutter would be perfectly camouflaged against the light coming down from the surface—except for an obvious dark oval "collar" around the shark's neck.

"Why the heck do that to a perfectly good camouflage pattern?" Edie asked herself. "Evolution doesn't make that kind of mistake."

Then, it hit her. Maybe, she thought, this dark oval looks like the shadow of a small fish to animals beneath it. If a dolphin or tuna came up to attack this "fish," the cookie cutter shark would have the perfect opportunity to grab on to it and scoop out a hunk of its flesh.

The more Edie thought about this, the more it made sense. The cookie cutter can make a strong vacuum with its mouth that would enable it to quickly attach itself to larger prey. Edie also had read that cookie cutter sharks often travel in schools. Therefore, a whole school of cookie cutter sharks would look like a tempting meal of tiny prey to dolphins, tunas, squids, and other predators swimming below. As Edie fit together her ideas with the work of other scientists, it all suddenly made sense. After 150 years, another mystery of bioluminescence was solved.

Mysterious Still

VER THE PAST THIRTY YEARS, Edie and other scientists have greatly expanded our knowledge of bioluminescence and how it helps animals survive. For every question scientists answer, however, a hundred others pop up.

One area Edie and her colleague Tammy Frank are trying to learn more about is the nightly migration of animals from the deep to shallower surface waters. This migration occurs throughout the world's oceans and is by far the most massive migration anywhere on Earth. Edie and Tammy are using the Johnson-Sea-Link to learn more about what triggers this behavior and exactly how migration influences the complex food web of the open ocean.

Edie also is one of many scientists who believes that it may be possible to use bioluminescence to evaluate how much life the ocean

OPPOSITE: Though the ocean is the most dominant feature on our planet, scientists are still making astonishing discoveries about its inhabitants.

produces. For decades, people have tried to measure the populations of fish that we eat, but we still have almost no idea of how many animals live in the sea. To help her evaluate such things, Edie has worked with James Case and other scientists to create instruments to measure bioluminescence. These instruments can be towed by a ship and will help us understand more about the quantity and distribution of life in the deep.

The Real Frontier

In this new century, scientists are making great strides in understanding the ocean and its marine life. However, what we *don't* know about bioluminescence and the ocean still far outweighs what we've learned so far. A big barrier for researchers is the high cost of studying the ocean. To operate the Johnson-Sea-Link submersible, for example, costs about $21,000 a day. Few scientists can get that kind of money to perform their research.

A bigger problem, though, is that the public still hasn't taken a large interest in the ocean. With the public's approval, our government spends billions of dollars a year to send people into outer space. We spend only a fraction of that on marine research. For the cost of sending the space shuttle into space *one time* (about $450 million dollars), scientists could fund two Johnson-Sea-Link crews and their support ships every day for the next twenty-nine years! Greater funding of ocean research will only happen, however, if the public demands it.

There are many reasons why we should.

For one thing, we depend on the ocean for our very survival. We obtain not only food from it, but also many raw materials that we use to make the products we need. The study of marine animals and plants has also led to the discovery of many new medicines and medical techniques. Safe, bioluminescent "tags" to identify cancerous tissues and other tissues in our bodies, for instance, have replaced the more dangerous radioactive substances that scientists used to use.

With public support, Edie and other marine biologists can continue their deep-sea explorations and help unlock more of the ocean's secrets.

Perhaps the biggest reason we should increase our study of the ocean, though, is that the ocean is *the* dominant feature on our planet. Most of the planet lies beneath the ocean waves, and yet we have only a vague idea of how the ocean functions, where ocean animals live, and how human activities are affecting the ocean. Every time Edie and other scientists explore the ocean depths, they discover something new. Only by continuing and expanding this exploration can we truly understand our planet, our fellow species, and how we fit into Earth's intricate web of life.

Glossary

ADAPTATION a physical or behavioral change that improves a species' chance of survival

BIOCHEMISTRY the study of the function and interactions of chemicals in the bodies of living things

BIOLOGIST a person who studies living things

BIOLUMINESCENCE the production of light by living organisms

COUNTERILLUMINATION the use of light to blend in with background light; a form of camouflage

DNA (DEOXYRIBONUCLEIC ACID) the material in living things that contains basic "instructions" for how cells and organisms grow and develop

ENZYME a protein that promotes or allows a chemical reaction without being used up itself

EVOLUTION the process by which species change over time through mutations that happen in their DNA; evolution is also what creates new species from older ones

PHOTOPHORES organs that produce light in animals

PLANKTON animals and plants, usually microscopic in size, that are carried by ocean currents and serve as important food for many larger animals

SUBMERSIBLE a small underwater craft often used for deep-sea research

To Learn More

Relatively little has been written about marine bioluminescence for young people, but several books that deal with fireflies, deep-sea animals, and marine bioluminescence include:

Collard, Sneed B., III. *The Deep-Sea Floor.* Watertown, MA: Charlesbridge Publishing, 2003.

Collard, Sneed B., III. *A Firefly Biologist at Work.* Danbury, CT: Franklin Watts, 2001.

Ganeri, Anita. *Creatures That Glow.* New York: Harry N. Abrams, 1995.

Presnall, Judith Janda. *Animals That Glow.* Danbury, CT: Franklin Watts, 1993.

Robison, Bruce, and Judith Connor. *The Deep Sea.* Monterey, CA: Monterey Bay Aquarium, 1999.

Widder, Edith A. *The Bioluminescence Coloring Book.* Fort Pierce, FL: Harbor Branch Oceanographic Institution, 1998.

Widder, Edith A. *Lucinda's Lamps: A Mermaid's Guide to Lights in the Sea.* (in press)

An outstanding video on bioluminescence is:

Marine Bioluminescence: Secret Lights in the Sea, produced by the Harbor Branch Oceanographic Institution, Fort Pierce, FL, 2000.

A good way to keep up with Dr. Widder's latest research on bioluminescence is to visit her Web sites at the Harbor Branch Oceanographic Institution. The addresses are: www.hboi.edu/marinesci/biolum.html *and* www.biolum.org

The Web site of the Harbor Branch Oceanographic Institution is also a great place to learn more about oceanography, marine biology, and the Johnson-Sea-Link submersibles. Its home page is http://www.hboi.ed

Index

About the Author

SNEED B. COLLARD III has written more than fifty books for young people. They include the popular picture books *Animal Dads, Leaving Home,* and *Animals Asleep* as well as in-depth science books such as *Monteverde: Science and Scientists in a Costa Rican Cloud Forest.* His books *The Forest in the Clouds* and *Beaks!* were both named Teacher's Choices by the International Reading Association, and many of his other titles have received similar recognition. Before beginning his writing career, Sneed graduated with honors in biology from the University of California at Berkeley. To research and photograph the SCIENCE ADVENTURES series, he visited Costa Rica's cloud forest, Australia's Great Barrier Reef, Zoo Atlanta, and the deep-sea floor. Sneed lives in Missoula, Montana, where he enjoys observing nature during long walks with his border collie, Mattie. His Web site is: www.sneedbcollardiii.com